MASTERING CONTENT CREATION

How to Grow and Monetize an Online Following

Liam Kimlin

Greystone Strategy

————————————————

Dedicated to you, for supporting me at the very
beginning of my career.

No matter where you purchased this book, any
review you leave is greatly appreciated! :)

————————————————

Table of Contents

Introduction

The exponential growth of online media has made it possible for thousands of people to become famous entertainers by posting creative content for millions to watch. Kids of all ages are posting pictures, videos, and articles of their favorite hobbies and turning into internet celebrities seemingly overnight. Recent studies show that **over 50%** of kids between the ages of 6 and 17 wish to be a 'YouTuber' or 'Blogger/Vlogger' when they grow up. Why wouldn't they? There's something magical about being able to be creative in front of a webcam in your room and earning enough to allow you to travel and work whenever you want. In fact, many might not even consider it 'work' if they're doing what they love.

The purpose of this book is to teach you everything you need to know about growing and marketing your online presence -- no matter what it is -- to maximize your chances of making it your career. From the outside looking in, it appears simple and easy to be a vlogger, YouTuber, or Instagram star: make content, post it online, get views, repeat. This, however, couldn't be any farther from the truth. While I admit it isn't a difficult job in the *traditional* sense of it being physically taxing (like construction work, for example), it does require much more thought and time than a typical job. Often, content creators work 7 days a week for hours on end filming, shooting photos, editing, brainstorming, and so on. Simply knowing this fact, combined with the insights provided in this book, will put you **one step ahead of your competition**. Learning these lessons early on in your online career will drastically improve your results, so long as you stick with it for the long-term.

- Chapter 1 -
Pick Your Passion

This first chapter may seem both intuitive and pointless, but I promise it is arguably the most important chapter of the book. The reason that this book starts with this topic is because it is the foundation that you will build your entire empire on; that foundation being the content you choose to make. Even if you think you know what type of content you would like to produce, I encourage you to start here because if this isn't done correctly it becomes **incredibly hard** to fix later down the line and many creators fail trying.

Before creating content, it's important to consider exactly what kind of content you'll create and how you can adapt it into other types of content. This means you'll need to figure out what your "bread and butter" is going to be – where your "main" content will be posted and what kinds of supplemental content you can create to support it. You could choose to be a YouTuber, Instagram model, Twitch Streamer, Blogger, Facebook Influencer, the list goes on. I'm sure as the social media landscape evolves, options could be added or removed from this list; for example, Vine was one that used to be on this list but is no longer, while you might be able to add Snapchat at the time of writing this.

As you grow your primary source of content, you can continue to expand into other areas of the internet to capture a greater number of followers, but it's important not to do this *too* soon. Stretching yourself thin and attempting to grow multiple projects all at once will take *a lot* of time and energy and, most importantly, you'll probably give up before any of them reach a substantial size. For example, if you choose to be a YouTuber, there are many natural routes you could take from there. You could build a website with a blog and have blog posts supplement your content, you could have a Twitch account to live stream to an audience, and you could also have an Instagram page where you post daily photographs. When you're first starting out, there are a few reasons to consider focusing on creating your best content for a single source:

1. The energy spent building high-quality content for multiple sites could be used to focus on your main source of content to much greater success

2. People are less likely to follow you on every social media site if you only have a few viewers or followers anyway

3. Growth on these platforms is usually more exponential than linear, so the same time put into one source will yield more results than put into many sources

4. Social media accounts are good to supplement your primary content source in the beginning rather than be a secondary standalone content source that requires attention and upkeep

Once you've figured out which platform you'd like to focus on, you then need to establish *what* you're going to post. This can be tricky for a few reasons, but it's good to have it outlined early on. First, you'll have to figure out what your content is going to be. This could mean you post fitness information, gaming videos, motivational pictures, vlogs of your day, or anything else you can think of. The rule of thumb is that if you're interested in it, there are likely thousands of others who are as well. Secondly, it must be something that you're truly passionate about. This point cannot be stressed enough... Often it takes months, if not years, to grow an online community. That means that you need to focus on gaining new followers **while also pleasing those who have previously followed you**. Most of the time that means sticking to the same genre of content for the duration of your time as a content creator. If you think that you can consistently create quality content for years **without** being passionate about it, you will be in for a rude awakening. Money and fame alone are almost never able to overcome this hurdle, as has been proven *many* times in the past. Creators with massive followings have faded away into obscurity because they either realized they don't love what they do, or they've lost their passion for it along the way, despite content creation being their primary source of income. Other times, mental health issues arise from creators who realize that they spend every day of their life doing something that they no longer like to do, yet they feel forced to do it because it's their job. Make sure to create content about something that you know you'll likely be passionate about for a very long time.

One big mistake that creators sometimes make is that they attempt to switch the focus of their content from one hobby to something entirely different, which usually doesn't work well. If this is going to be done, it must be done elegantly and slowly while gaining feedback from your fan base. As stated earlier in this chapter, it isn't impossible to do, but it's difficult to pull off without people losing interest. Typically, you would need to either shift your content to a topic that your audience also cares about, or you would need a very large and loyal fan base to stick with you even after your switch. One of the most famous examples of this is the content of the biggest YouTuber (at the time of writing this)

PewDiePie. He grew his channel and his brand by posting gameplay videos, and now he hardly plays any games at all. He was only able to switch the focus of his content because he made *even higher quality videos* after he stopped posting about video games, combined with the fact that he has a massive audience that is loyal to him. It also helps that the content he creates now is something that his existing fan base would still consider entertaining or funny, despite it not being the original reason why they subscribed to him in the first place.

In summary, no matter what you choose to make your content about, make sure that it is something that you'll have a passion for in the future. This may be easier said than done, so give it some thought. It's better to spend a day or two *really* thinking about this than spending a year building your audience in the wrong direction.

- Chapter 2 -
Defining Yourself

One term used a lot in both business and marketing is **"Unique Selling Proposition"**. The Unique Selling Proposition (or USP) is used to define what sets them apart from their competition. It essentially answers the question *"Why would somebody buy from us and not our competition?"* As you can imagine, having a well-defined USP is key to building a long-lasting business. If you are just like everybody else, then there's no reason for people to buy your product, and the same is true for content creators.

Having a USP with regards to content creation is as vital as it is for any other type of business, especially these days. With hundreds of thousands of people around the globe competing to grow their online audience, it's crucial to stand out. If, for example, you decided last chapter that you were going to make a YouTube channel centered around the military shooter videogame series "Call of Duty", you now must ask yourself how you'll be different from everybody else doing that. Why would somebody want to watch *you* over all the other people posting videos about Call of Duty? Will you have better editing? Do you think you're one of the best players out there? Will you post more videos at a consistent rate than everybody else? This may sound more complicated than it is, and it's something that a lot of people over-think.

One key to defining your USP is one that people overlook when they analyze what makes them different, and the answer is **you**. No matter what content you decide to post, you yourself are unique. This may sound cliché or lame, but it's 100% true. As a content creator, if you are open, honest, and genuine with your audience, they will be able to connect with you *much* better than somebody else who is more "robotic" with how they run their channel. In fact, to support my claim, the word "You" is **literally in the name of the site "<u>You</u>Tube"**. The real reason why YouTube has grown so substantially over the last decade is because of the individual creators being relatable, personable, and genuine; all things that are missing from big-budget television shows with scripts and actors.

Understanding that *you* are likely the reason that people will continue to come back to consume your content is also a major key in figuring out what new types of content you could create. You may have heard (or thought to yourself) that "everything has already been done before!" with regards to coming up with "original" content. While it is true that it's difficult to come up with an idea that is truly original, you don't always have to. If you see a cool idea for content that was already done before, don't feel ashamed doing something similar. After all, even if it's been done before, it hasn't been done *by you* before. While it's always nice to be a "trendsetter" in the industry (and often being the first on a wave will generate the most reward), don't think that you **must**. Some people may just want to see you post content about what's going on in your industry or the current trends of the time. Adding your own personality to something that's already been done will still be entertaining to your audience.

Infusing yourself and your personality into your content aside, there are still other ways to define yourself and your USP. One way is to figure out what *other* people are doing in your industry. It's likely that you were inspired to start posting content about your passion on the internet by somebody else that you saw doing it successfully. Start by examining your idols, and then branch out and examine their competition. What are these people doing that defines who they are? Are there any similar themes or traits? Are certain themes *oversaturating the industry?* More importantly, **is what they're doing actually working?** Try to take what's working for others and incorporate it into your own content in a unique way. Additionally, make sure to *actually support* your USP. If you start a tech blog with the tagline "The First to Report on Tech News You

Care About!" (lame, I know, but you get the point) *make sure that you are first...* at least some of the time. If you're constantly reposting articles you find elsewhere, then what "defines" you (the fact that you're the first with the news) is just a false claim that people won't believe.

Perhaps your USP is that you can form a rock-solid brand image that *really* stands out. For example, while thousands of people would post cooking videos to YouTube, Facebook, and Instagram, "Tasty" videos by Buzzfeed still rose up above the competition. One reason for this is because all the videos had a unifying theme and style that was unique to only them. Of course, because of their success there are many who now imitate them, but the point remains that it was *easy* to tell when you were watching a "Tasty" video. Generating this kind of brand image will undoubtably set you apart from your competition and could easily be a major part of your USP.

Finally, consider if it's possible to fuse your other hobbies into your content to make it unique. Taking another example from the culinary side of the internet, Rosanna Pansino is well-known for infusing both her hobbies and pop culture events into her recipes. She won't simply make cupcakes, she'll make cupcakes inspired by Star Wars. What's more, she won't do this randomly either, she'll post that type of video right around the launch of a new Star Wars movie. If you have multiple hobbies, ask yourself how they could overlap in a creative way.

- Chapter 3 -

Targeting the Right Market

One incredibly useful piece of information to know when creating content is **the type of person interested in it**. If you're attempting to create content for a living, you want to maximize the amount of return you get on everything that you invest your time into. Knowing the demographic most likely to view and enjoy the content posted in your niche is key to maximizing your efforts. This is easily figured out as an established creator because all social media sites offer *some* sort of analytics relating to your content, but what about when you're just starting out?

There are many ways to figure out your target demographic if you're willing to invest some time into doing the research. The most simple and straightforward way to begin to gauge what your demographic looks like is by examining the people that you know. Do you know of anybody who is interested in your topic, hobby, or passion? These people could be friends, family, coworkers, classmates, and everybody in between. What do these people look like? How old are they, and what do they do for a living? Taking a moment to consider these questions could yield some useful data moving forward. For example, if you want to build a following for your Instagram page that focuses on puppies, and you realize that 75% of the people you know that love puppies are women, then that could be significant when you advertise your content later down the line. That data could also help you curate your content to focus more on women and the other things that women tend to like. Why waste your time targeting men if most of your followers are women anyway?

Aside from analyzing the people you encounter daily, another way to get a general idea of what your demographic could look like is by observing your competition. Go to the comments section of other people posting similar content to yours and see what the people there look like. Those who post comments and engage with content are the exact kinds of people you want anyway, so this method is not to be underestimated. Take note of as much data as you can, including their approximate age, sex, race, hobbies, location, and anything else you can find. When attempting to define an age bracket, try to keep it within a five year window. Going beyond that is much less focused and the people on either end of the spectrum likely won't have much in common.

They say in school that Google is your best friend, and that is unsurprisingly the case with demographic research as well. If you'd like to be thorough with your information collection, you can use Google AdWords Display Planner in combination with Google Trends. The AdWords Display Planner will allow you to see the age and the "device used" of people searching for content in your industry. Google Trends will offer insight into the most popular locations for your content, giving you country, state, and city data over a timespan. The best part is that both services are free if you have a Google account and are super easy to use. It's important to mention, however, that this data still isn't going to be better than *actual* data that you are going to collect through your own analytics. This is meant to show you the big picture of the industry your content belongs to but won't necessarily align perfectly with your audience once you get the ball rolling.

As a last resort, you could split-test cheap Google or Facebook ads and see which does better. This might sound complicated or risky but it's straightforward. First, pick a piece of your content that you're proud of or that you think is some of your best work. Next, create a Google, Facebook, or Instagram advertisement for that piece of content and target an age demographic that you think would be most likely to enjoy it. When promoting the ad, set a small budget of $10 or $15 for the entire duration of the ad campaign. Once that's finished, create a *second* ad promoting the exact same piece of content and target another age demographic that's different than your first. Without changing other variables, including the amount you spend, you should get a general idea of which demographic responds better to your content. Again, this data might not be as reliable as the actual analytics you get through your social media pages, but it can supplement it. Even if the data you get is lackluster or unclear, at least you were able to expose your content to a new audience!

Using a combination of the methods listed in this chapter, you should be able to get a good idea of what demographic will likely be most interested in your content. Equally as important as this initial research is continuing to check in on your analytics periodically. As time goes on, you'll have a much better idea of what type of person is enjoying your content because you'll have a lot more data to back it up.

The final thing that needs to be said about demographic data is this: content that is "family friendly" seems to do better in the long run than controversial and offensive content. If you're overly vulgar and go for "shock value" with your content, consider what doors might open to you if you took a less harsh approach. Sites like YouTube and Facebook actively age-restrict content from minors when they feel like it would be inappropriate for them. That means that one of the biggest demographics is instantly unable to view your content, and that will make growing your business harder. While this is by no means an "absolute must", it's just something to consider. Many content creators grew to the size they're at *because* they were offensive and crude, so it just depends on your content specifically.

- Chapter 4 -
Content Creation

Now that you've decided what your passion is that you'll create content about, how you're going to do it differently than others, and who you plan to make content for, it's finally time to get to work. As mentioned in the first chapter, the content that you choose to create and where it gets posted is entirely up to you. There are endless possibilities when it comes to this step in the process, so really, it's up to you to create what you're inspired to. Since it would be impossible to go in depth about every single niche, industry, passion, and hobby, this chapter will focus on explaining each of the primary platforms that people choose to grow on, as well as the equipment needed to do so. As you grow your following and your business, you could easily branch out to more than one of these platforms, but to start it would be smarter to stick with just one.

A popular choice for many social media stars of the last few years is **YouTube**, a video sharing website owned by Google that allows its users to upload as much video content as they want to their channel for free (so long as it falls within their community guidelines). The video content on YouTube is literally endless, with users posting hundreds of thousands of hours of video every single day. Getting started on YouTube is easy but standing out and growing your channel is where it begins to get difficult.

Many people believe that they need essentially a small home studio to start growing on YouTube, complete with an expensive camera, microphone, lighting equipment, green screen, and everything else their favorite YouTuber uses. This is not true at all, and many videos that have millions of views were filmed with nothing more than a cheap camera or cellphone. It *is* important to improve your equipment as you go, slowly acquiring things that will make your content higher quality, better looking, and more impressive, but there's no need to spend thousands of dollars before you even begin. It's more important to make sure that you learn how to create content and get a feel for whether you truly enjoy being a YouTuber or not. Start small with what you have and improve as you go along. Some content will require different equipment than others, but most will require at least a camera or webcam and a microphone. If you're attempting to be a vlogger, starting with your smartphone camera is enough until you can grow to a size where your quality needs an upgrade. If you're making videos from your computer, you can get a cheap HD webcam for around $60. Similarly, before buying a studio microphone for hundreds of dollars, consider the fact that a small microphone that costs less than $15 will likely still be far superior to the on-board microphone of your webcam, cellphone, or computer. Again, making these purchases in small increments eases the financial burden and allows you to learn as you go. Additionally, many types of videos require editing that is usually best done on a computer. It might seem like you *must* have a good computer to edit videos, but this isn't always the case. If your computer is at least good enough to *run* editing software, it's usually enough to get the job done. Older or slower computers will take longer to "render" a video (which means turn your edited clips into a final product) but timing the rendering process correctly will make this less noticeable. For example, a good computer might render a video in 30 minutes whereas an older computer might take 5 hours. While this difference is drastic, it's worth mentioning that you could easily just wait to render the video until you go to bed so that way when you wake up in the morning, it will be finished and won't inconvenience you.

When it comes to software, there are a few things to consider. Typically, you will need at least video editing software to put your clips and effects together. The most common choices are Adobe Premiere Pro, Final Cut Pro (Macs only), Sony Vegas, and Camtasia Studio. In reality, most professionals use one of the first two while the second two seem to be used more scarcely by creators in the video game niche. Obviously, learning how to edit videos is important, but that skill is much better learned by watching tutorials instead of reading about it here. For now, just focus on picking software and getting familiar with it so that way you can get better (and faster) at editing with enough practice. If you can't afford the software listed above, there are many free options out there, some of which come pre-installed on your computer like iMovie does with Macs.

Another piece of software that is usually important is one that can edit photos. Adobe Photoshop pretty much dominates this industry, but you could easily get away with free software like GIMP or Paint.net if you're just getting started. The reason you should use a photo editing software is because it will allow you to create high quality thumbnail pictures for your YouTube videos. A "thumbnail" is the image that accompanies your video on YouTube; the one people see before they click your video. In a way, a thumbnail to a YouTube video is like the cover to a book. It's important to know that while many say not to judge a book by its cover, almost everybody does. This means that having a high-quality, enticing thumbnail will drastically improve the odds of somebody choosing to watch your video. As with video editing, photo editing is much better learned by watching tutorial videos and getting hands-on practice. While a "good thumbnail" will vary depending on your niche, here are a few general rules that you can follow that should set you up for success:

1. Make sure your images are high definition, preferably with dimensions of 1280x720 because that's what YouTube itself recommends at the time of writing this. Ensure that the image isn't blurry and that the text in your image can be read **even when it's smaller on YouTube.** Forgo cool, custom fonts for ones that are easily readable.

2. Bright, warm colors attract the eye much more than cool colors. This is the reason why stop signs and stop lights are red. Having colors like red, yellow, and orange in your thumbnail will attract more attention than one with blue or purple.

3. People are more likely to click on videos if somebody's face is in the thumbnail. While this seems like a weird psychological trick, it's supported by data so try to take

advantage of it by including a picture of the subject of your video in your thumbnail.

4. Make sure to keep in mind that YouTube puts the video's length in the bottom right corner of your thumbnail, so avoid putting any text or important information down there.

Aside from just creating thumbnails for your videos, creating a banner and icon for your channel is also important. Having custom designs on your channel will look more professional than the default one and shows potential subscribers that you take YouTube seriously. If you don't feel comfortable making your thumbnails or channel artwork in the beginning, you could pay somebody online to do it for you. While editing photos is a vital skill when it comes to growing your business, many sites like Fiverr.com exist that allow you to find a professional to do it for you while you get better. This is not a good long-term solution because the cost will add up quickly, plus learning a new skill on your own is always better. If anything, purchase channel graphics and icons from a professional and create your own thumbnails so you can learn as you go.

Eventually, you'll be comfortable enough to create everything on your channel from scratch.

With knowing how to create, edit, and upload videos, combined with the skill of crafting eye-catching thumbnails and channel graphics, you now know the bulk of what you need to know. Creating content regularly will give you enough practice to get better, and those skills can be applied to many other online businesses.

Being an **Instagram Influencer** is also another popular way to build a large following online. What's interesting about Instagram is that you don't necessarily need much more than just a smartphone that takes good pictures and videos, but you need to also post more content than on YouTube.

The first thing to establish when building your Instagram presence is your bio. Instagram is very limiting with what you can do with your bio, so making the most of it is crucial. Make sure to clearly state what you want to convey to your followers in only a few words. Try adding a few emojis to make it look more visually appealing as well, but **do not** go overboard with them. The most important part of your bio is going to be the link to your website, which is the only place where you can put a link that is clickable on Instagram. This link should either go to another place where your followers can view your content, your own website, or a page that clearly lists your other social media links. Related to this is the *type* of Instagram account you have. If you are going to take Instagram seriously, turning your account into an Instagram Business account is crucial. This free feature will allow you to get even more analytics about your followers and who is engaging with your posts. This goes hand-in-hand with the previous chapter, which made it clear that the more data you have at your disposal, the better. It will tell you the best times to post your content, the demographics of your audience, and much more.

As mentioned before, posting on Instagram should be more frequent than YouTube uploads. Top Instagram influencers post between one and two times per day, and that's definitely a good number to shoot for. Instagram is much faster paced than YouTube, so it requires *constant* interaction, engagement, and posting. Don't just post *anything* though, make sure it fits within your niche or passion. Each image should be as creative as the last, because if quality decreases people will stop caring about what you're posting altogether. It's important to know that Instagram has its own algorithm that determines what each individual user is most interested in. Every time they open the application, the newest posts are shown in order of what Instagram thinks you'll like most. Naturally, the accounts that you interact with most often will likely show up first. Having lots of engagement on a consistent basis will ensure that you continue to stay relevant to your followers.

Another technique that top Instagram influencers use is the creation of a unifying theme across all posts. Most brands and influencers will stick to the same filter for every post, that way they all share something in common and look nice when presented together on the profile page. This method is a way to make a photograph look uniquely *yours*. Some influencers even have their own custom filters that they save as presets on their computer in a program called Adobe Lightroom. This takes a bit more time, effort, skill, and knowledge of photography, but it could pay off by having your pictures look like nobody else's on the platform. On a more basic level, start by just including similar colors and subjects in all your posts. If your Instagram focuses primarily on food, too many posts about unrelated things will cause engagement to decrease over time.

Another key to Instagram is to post a combination of videos, photos, and stories. Having a variety means there's more for your followers to engage with, plus it gives you more creativity over what you post. Not only do videos get more comments on average than photos, the engagement overall is increasing year over year. Stories on the other hand provide you with a way to interact with your audience more directly and offer a way to update them often without posting too frequently. It's better to post 10 things a day to your story than 10 things a day on your actual profile, because most of them will likely not be of the highest quality. Not only that, but stories allow you to integrate a rating system, have your audience answer questions, and give them a poll to ask them what they think. This is even more data that you have at your disposal!

Finally, no matter what you post, be sure to include as many hashtags as you can. Instagram will limit you to 30 so be sure to make the most of them. Hashtags are a way to group your image in with other images of that hashtag, effectively exposing it to thousands of people who may have never heard of you otherwise. Essentially, hashtags are keywords that you can add to your posts so that it will appear on the "Discover" page of people that it would be relevant to. It should go without saying that it's important to choose at least a handful of hashtags that have at least a few hundred thousand posts in order to maximize your exposure. If you have 30 hashtags and none of them have ever been used before, the odds of somebody looking it up are highly improbable. On the other end of the spectrum, if you *only* include the most popular hashtags, your post will quickly be drowned out by the massive amounts of competition for that hashtag. With that being said, having a balance is best; pick some specific hashtags for your post and then add some even more popular ones to cover all of the bases.

Moving on to our next platform of content creation, **Twitch** is a live streaming platform that is *mostly* associated with gaming. While this section will reference Twitch as the platform in question, these tips and rules can be applied to pretty much any livestreaming site like UStream, YouTube Gaming, Smashcast.tv, Periscope, etc. Users on these platforms can create a channel for free and, with the right software, broadcast themselves playing games, listening to music, talking to their audience, and much more. Twitch also shows a live feed of users who are commenting so that they can interact with the person who is broadcasting.

A few things are necessary to begin live streaming on Twitch, some of which are the same as YouTube. The primary thing that all Twitch professionals have is a decent computer capable of live streaming their game of choice. Without this, you're relatively limited with what you can do on Twitch. Video game consoles these days like the PlayStation 4 and Xbox One allow you to live stream directly from your game, but this method is a bit more amateur and doesn't typically allow your audience to see or hear you unless you have specific accessories for that console. If audiences can't interact with you, they'll quickly get bored and go view somebody else playing the same game. The interaction component that comes with having a good computer due to your ability to have broadcasting software that will customize your streaming experience, but more on this later.

Along with a decent computer and a source of content (typically a video game), it's recommended to have a webcam and microphone. This combination is essential for reasons mentioned above; you want to be as interactive as possible with your audience while you're streaming. A decent webcam and mic combo can run you as little as $70, but of course upgrading as you go will improve your stream quality. As mentioned when discussing starting a YouTube channel, upgrade these pieces of equipment over time instead of dropping thousands of dollars up front. No matter which webcam or microphone you have, viewers prefer watching a streamer that they can see and hear because otherwise it would be like watching a football or basketball game without the commentators.

One factor that can't be overlooked when streaming is the speed of your internet connection, particularly your upload speed. The speed of your internet can be figured out easily and for free simply by Googling "internet speed test". Without enough bandwidth, you will be forced to stream in lower quality and will likely have technical issues like lag, dropped frames, and your stream shutting down intermittently. Again, these issues will give your viewers a bad experience when attempting to watch you, and they'll likely get frustrated and watch somebody else. This reason alone is sometimes why people living in more rural areas have trouble live streaming; fast internet service simply isn't an option for them or it's far too expensive. The good news is that you don't need to stream in full 1080p with 60 frames per second to grow on Twitch. Having 720p streams with 30 frames per second is preferred by many viewers because sometimes *it's the viewer with slow internet*. If you only broadcast in ultra HD, some viewers might not be able to load your stream in the first place.

As you grow on Twitch and get partnered with them, options become available to give your audience the choice for which quality they'd prefer to watch you in. Until then, streaming in a quality that most people can view is important.

As with a YouTube channel, having graphics on your Twitch channel will make you appear more professional and committed. Twitch allows you to have a custom banner as well as custom tiles beneath your stream called "panels". These both present opportunities to make your channel look and feel the way you want it to; you can present yourself and your brand in the light that you want new and returning viewers to see you in. Again, making these custom graphics for your channel should be done in either Adobe Photoshop, GIMP, or Paint.net, but you can also outsource this part as well. By now, you might be realizing that having a basic understanding of how to edit and create graphics is a universally useful skill, and it is! Instead of constantly outsourcing this part of the process, really take some time to learn the basics so you can avoid spending too much while also learning a valuable skill. Once you've grown to a large enough size to where Twitch or YouTube is your full-time job, paying a designer to make professional graphics becomes much more justifiable.

Finally, if you're streaming from a computer, you'll need streaming software that was mentioned before. The most popular ones are OBS Studio and XSplit. OBS (meaning Open Broadcasting Software) is free and straight forward to use, plus there are tons of tutorials online for how to set it up perfectly given your internet speed. XSplit has a highly intuitive interface and offers great features but also has a subscription cost associated with it. The reason software is needed is because it essentially packages your broadcast and tells your computer what account on Twitch to broadcast it to. Additionally, this software allows you to layer different video sources, images, audio sources, and more all on the same screen. This allows you to have banner overlays for your broadcasts that show off your social media links, your highest scores, most active viewers, and so on. You can go very in depth with streaming software in combination with StreamLabs, another free program that allows for even more viewer interaction. As with editing for YouTube, learning how to use these programs simply takes a bit of practice and some time watching a few tutorials when you get stuck.

The most traditional way of growing a following on the internet is by creating your own **Blog**. Back before people posted high-definition videos to YouTube, before live streaming of video games was possible, and before models proved that Instagram was a viable career, bloggers grew large followings because of their continuous output of content. Essentially, a blog is a website that you create and can then post articles, content, and updates to. These days, creating a blog is *super* easy, very affordable, and you don't need to know how to code anything either. After the initial setup of the website, posting a new piece of content is almost as easy as posting to a site like Facebook; you simply type out your content, make it look how you want, and maybe add a picture or two. Despite blogging being the "grandfather" of all content creators online, it remains one of the most viable ways to create a following.

The first thing you'll need to create your own blog is a place to put it. Traditionally, the most professional blogs have their own website, but you could also start your blog on wordpress.com, Tumblr, Blogger, or any other free website online. As you move forward though, it will likely be necessary to move your content to its own domain name (what you type into the top bar of your browser; "Google.com" is Google's domain name). Creating your own website sounds a lot harder than it is, especially because of the variety of free Content Management Systems (CMS) out there that you can install essentially with the click of a button.

The easy way to create your own website with its own domain name is to use a website like WordPress, Wix, SquareSpace, Weebly, or one of the many others available across the internet. These providers will not only give you a free place to put your blog and manage the content within it, but they will also move all the data seamlessly to its own custom domain name, continue to manage its content, and host the site every month for a fee. Of course, the fee for them to do it for you is higher than if you were to do it yourself, but for those who can't be bothered with learning how to do it, this might be the best option. Otherwise, it would be better to buy a domain name and hosting package from a site like GoDaddy or HostGator and then install a content management system yourself (again, essentially the click of a button) and proceed in that way. Usually, sites like GoDaddy and HostGator have incredibly cheap introductory packages to acquire new customers like you! Whichever route you choose, it's just important that eventually you have your own standalone website to post your content to.

As with the previous methods, having custom-made graphics is important to make your website look unique, clean, and professional. By now, you should understand the importance of using Photoshop or GIMP! Thankfully, much of your website design can be established with Themes, which are pre-built website structures and designs that a web developer will package and sell (or give away) on sites like WordPress. The use of a theme in combination with a CMS like WordPress is the reason why you don't necessarily need to know how to code to make a beautiful and functional website; the structure has already been coded for you. As mentioned before, themes can either be given away for free or can be sold for a fee. No matter which theme you choose, just make sure to customize it to your liking with some graphics that are branded to your industry.

The process for running a blog is straightforward: you post content and articles to your blog a few times per week that provide value to your readers. With that in mind, it goes a bit more in-depth than that when you're really trying to pull in new readers. Similar to how you might entice people to view your YouTube videos, a strategic title (and sometimes thumbnail) for your article is crucial. Not only that but incorporating Search Engine Optimization (SEO) techniques in your articles will help rank your content on search engines. For example, if you have a new blog about making your own candles, your first few articles aren't likely to show up on Google, Yahoo, or Bing if somebody searches for "How to make candles". There are techniques that you can use to increase the probability of this, however, and mastering the ins and outs of SEO will be vital to growing your following as effectively as possible. One vital thing you must learn to do is getting into the habit of incorporating keywords into your articles. Keywords are the things that people are typing in when they're searching for something in a search engine, and function *kind of* like hashtags on Instagram, but are built into the content. Using our previous example, a few keywords for a website that talks about making your own candles could be "candle making", "how to make candles", "DIY candle making", "homemade candles", and so on. Unlike Instagram, however, these keywords need to be seamlessly integrated into the article itself. Posting an article as normal and then adding a massive block of text at the end with thousands of keywords will *not* likely trick any search engines because they've learned over time what a good and what a bad website looks like. The reason that Google is so popular is because of how **good** it is; usually the user has the information they need in the first few search results. If Google didn't prioritize websites that it thought not only fit what the person was searching for, but also was a genuinely *good* website, people would find it less useful and go to a different search engine. Google isn't more popular than Yahoo and Bing because "it just is", it's because it's algorithm and filter are (arguably) *better* than that of its competitors. This means that not only does your content need to be good, it must be very relevant to what people are searching for. As with everything discussed so far, there is no secret or shortcut that can be put in this book; learning how to do this effectively will only come with practice and some video tutorials online where needed.

Finally, a key component to having a successful blog is a mailing list. A mailing list is a list of emails that your site visitors will give you willingly in exchange for something in return. Typically, people will sign up for a mailing list when they subscribe to a newsletter (a weekly email that you send to subscribers to provide value to them), get a free download after signing up, get a free consultation, or any creative combination you can think of. No matter what you give in return, it's important that you establish the mailing list feature early on, otherwise you're missing what makes growing a blog truly great. Many services will help you build your mailing list, but the few that people typically praise are MailChimp, iContact, Constant Contact, Marketing 360, and HubSpot, just to name a few. These services will allow you to connect your website offer to your account with them where they will store your growing list of email subscribers. Once established, you can program it to automatically send a welcome email as well as weekly content that you want your followers to see. This is how you'll email all your subscribers at once, instead of having to do it manually. This component of having a blog cannot be stressed enough, and video tutorials on how to set this up are relatively straightforward.

It's worth mentioning that another place to build your following apart from YouTube, Twitch, Instagram, or blogs is **Facebook**. Some Facebook Fan pages have millions of likes that garner attention from people and brands around the world. Typically, the pages that grow on Facebook organically (that aren't brands or celebrities elsewhere) are ones about a topic or hobby, not just a random person or business like on Instagram, YouTube, or Twitch. This means general niche pages are more likely to grow, so making a page about your hobby in general might be your best bet.

While these five platforms are the most popular for building a following online, as mentioned before, they aren't the only ones. The internet is massive, ever-changing, and certain platforms might exist in some countries and not others. Regardless, the information for the platforms mentioned in this section can likely be used and applied to many other platforms across the internet, even ones that have yet to be developed. What's important is developing the basic skills needed to create high-quality content, as well as getting the hang of creating content regularly. Once you've mastered this workflow, you can essentially apply it to any platform moving forward.

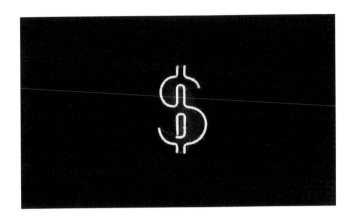

- Chapter 5 -
Opportunity for Income

Now that we've discussed how to make content for each of these platforms, it's time to talk about how they can earn revenue. The important thing to know about making money by being a content creator is that it typically follows an exponential growth curve. This means that for a while, the amount that you make will be virtually nothing, but over time it will grow at an increasing rate. For most internet entrepreneurs, a lot of the work is done up front before they make any money, but it will compound over time so that they end up making money off work that they've done in the past. In a way, you can think of each piece of content you create as a little worker you've summoned to do work for you, even when you're offline, sleeping, or doing whatever you want. The fruits of their individual labor at first will be almost nothing, but when you have hundreds (or thousands) of them working at the same time, the pennies they make start turning into gold. The best part is that as you grow your fanbase, your workers get more and more productive!

The most traditional way people associate with making money off creating content is through **advertising revenue** (we'll call it ad revenue). This form of passive income is most effective for YouTube channels and websites, although some Twitch streamers have ads as well. Ad revenue is most commonly obtained by creating an AdSense account with Google (it's free) and then linking this account to either your YouTube channel or website. On YouTube, this means that there will be small video ads that run before, during, or after your videos. The more people watching, the more money you make. Typically, you can expect between $1 and $2 per 1,000 views, and that ratio is called your **CPM** or Cost Per Mille (mille in Latin means Thousand).

While that may seem incredibly low (because it is, relative to television), consider what happens down the line when you have a substantial fanbase: posting 3 videos per week that get 50,000 views each is equivalent to $225 per week... *on top of the views all your old videos are still getting* (assuming an average of $1.50 CPM). Now this still might not be a lot of money, but it's enough to be substantial to most low to middle class people. Additionally, that doesn't consider other ways you can harmlessly monetize your content (more on this later) and the fact that your growth will, as mentioned before, likely be more exponential than linear. What happens when you get a higher CPM? Or post more videos per week? Or you get 100,000 views per video? Or 250,000?

I hope by now you're beginning to see the picture. A small CPM can still compound into a substantial living. On websites and blogs, this works in a similar fashion. Space on your website will be used to post banner ads by Google. With that being the case, the more ads on your site the more money you make, but *not really*. Consider how likely you are to return to a website that is *covered* in advertisements... probably not likely.

This means that you need to experiment with how many ads you want to run on your site (if any at all) so that people don't feel like their experience is being hindered by constant ads. The good news is that if you don't want to run ads on your website, there are still plenty of other options for making money from it.

Another common way to make money on any platform with a following is by posting **sponsored content**. Unlike ad revenue, which can be set up right from the beginning, sponsored content is only an opportunity for people farther along in their career because it requires a decent sized following. Essentially, sponsored content is accomplished by having a company pay you to promote their product, service, or content. This promotion could be in the form of a YouTube video, Instagram post, Blog article, or any other form of content that you can create. Sometimes, smaller creators can get free products in exchange for promotions, but getting paid real money is usually only for creators with thousands of engaged followers. With that being said, there are a few key things to know when creating sponsored content:

1. Don't have too many sponsored posts. Your viewers will start to get fed up if they realize that every other post is just your attempt at promoting products to them. They subscribed or followed you for *you* and your content, not to be advertised to.

2. Only accept sponsorships from companies and products that you personally enjoy and that you think your audience could benefit from. This should go without saying but accepting promotions only from companies you truly support will lead to a better experience for everybody. If you get paid to promote something your audience won't like, then they'll get upset that you're "selling out", and the company that paid you will get upset that they didn't see a good return on their investment (because your audience won't likely buy). Additionally, if you yourself don't like what you're promoting then the promotion is just a lie. In the world of building an audience, the last thing you want to do is to lie to them, because then the trust they have in you is gone.

3. Integrate the sponsorship in a creative, entertaining way. Simply posting about how much you enjoy a product or service is just an advertisement and it won't be very effective. *Actually* using the product or service in a video or post that you already had planned (or planned around the promotion) will get people wondering where they can purchase it as well. The idea is to make the content feel organic and natural, as if it is something you would have posted with or without the sponsorship.

4. You **must** make it clear that you are getting paid for a sponsored post. It is illegal to encourage your fan base to buy a product or service if you don't reveal to them that you are getting compensated to do so.

With that being said, this is probably the best time to talk about how to get a sponsorship. First off, it's important to know what businesses are looking for when they look for a person to sponsor. You need to have decent engagement on your content, a solid following, and sufficient branding. It needs to be apparent that you can provide the company value by being sponsored by them; what you bring to the table should be clear.

Once that is out of the way, understand that there are at least three types of sponsorships. The first, which is best for small to medium sized followings, is one where the company provides you a free product or sample in exchange for a content piece about them. Typically, they will want you to say good, honest things about their product, and encourage your following to check them out. These types of sponsorships aren't too difficult to get if you're working with a brand-new company, and it shouldn't come as a surprise if small companies reach out to you via email to inquire about you doing a product promotion for them.

The second type of sponsorship is an affiliate sponsorship with a company. This is perfect for really any sized following, and its effectiveness depends on how strong of a fan base you have, as well as how good the product is. The way this works is the company gives you a unique discount code that, when used at checkout, will provide the buyer with a discount on whatever they're purchasing. The percentage that the buyer saves goes to you for promoting the product!

Obviously, the more people who buy using your link, the more money you'll make.

The third type of sponsorship is one where you actually get paid by a company to promote their product or service. This is best for people with larger followings. Essentially, a company will pay you for a promotional campaign that you run for a given amount of time. This could be a one-time promotion for a single piece of content, a monthly promotion where you plug the product once a month, or any other arrangement that benefits both parties.

How hard it is to get a sponsorship will depend on how big of an engaged following you have, as well as how hard it is to get a sponsorship from the particular company you're trying to get one from. With that being said, attempting to get a sponsorship from a giant corporation as a small content creator is never going to happen because it isn't in the company's best interest to give you money or free products for relatively nothing in exchange.

Now that you have an idea of what kinds of sponsorships are available, next you need to figure out how to get one. The best place to start is Google, where you can search for companies within your niche. If you only have a small following, try to look for newer companies or startups in your niche because they're more likely to agree to sponsor your content. Once you've made a list of all the various companies that you think a sponsorship would make sense from, next you'll look for their contact information. Typically, this information is easily found at the top or bottom of their website or on their social media pages. Next, send them an email that is *short and sweet*, explaining why you think it would be mutually beneficial for you to work together. Include a few key metrics about your fan base, such as how large it is, average number of views on your content, and what percentage of your following is male versus female. Make sure your proposal is grammatically correct and *do not* send out a template email where you simply replace the company name. The person reading it will instantly know that you didn't take the time to really think up a personalized proposal for them and they'll think you're just sending that email to any company in hopes of getting something for free. Make your proposal personalized and high quality.

If you're not sure what companies you should approach for sponsorships, there are websites called sponsorship platforms that will help you with this process. Essentially a sponsorship platform is a hub where sponsors will go when they're actively looking for content creators to promote their brand. Simply make an account on the site, link your content, and browse the available sponsorships. You can make a proposal right through the website and the company will either approve or deny your request depending on if they think it would be the right fit for them. Some good sponsorship platforms are FameBit, Webfluential, AspireIQ (formally Revfluence), NeoReach, and Grape Vine Logic.

While sponsored content encourages sales of a company's goods or services, **selling your own products** is another way that you can make money by having a large following. Usually this is most profitable if you already have a large fan base, but it's not difficult to set up early on as well. Products you can sell largely depend on what your hobby, industry, or niche is. A lot of creators choose to have a line of apparel and accessories because it's a good way for fans to show support for their content. Additionally, it's not very difficult to have a design made for a shirt and then outsource the printing and shipping of the merchandise to an online company for a fee. Besides clothes, some creators write books, sell access to a premium feature on their website, and even help produce their own video games. Really, the sky is the limit with this method, you just need to be creative and make sure it's something that your fans would want to purchase. This form of earning money from a fanbase is unlike the previous two because it usually requires more time, effort, and sometimes money, to get off the ground.

A fourth method that you can use to earn money by having a large following online is through **donations**. This one may seem farfetched, but thousands of people make a living off donations from fans. Typically, this form of monetization is found on Twitch, but the business model can also be used by others through platforms like Patreon. Essentially, people who live stream on Twitch can set up a way to have donations appear on screen *live* during the broadcast, followed by a message from the donator (if they include one). Not only that, but sometimes top donators get displayed prominently on the screen until their "rank" is overtaken by somebody else. Plus, some creators have animations, sounds, and events that occur when somebody donates to encourage them to do so. For individuals that don't live stream, Patreon is a way to get donations from fans in exchange for special perks. Some creators offer content exclusively to patrons, others allow patrons to influence their next content upload, and most shout out their patrons in their videos, on their websites, and wherever else they can. Whatever the perks may be, sometimes fans just want to give back to somebody who entertains them regularly as a way of saying thanks. While it may seem odd at first that strangers on the internet want to give you money, consider the fact that you give them hours of entertainment and knowledge for free! They appreciate that and want to return the favor in any small way they can. That being the case, consider donations as an additional way to get revenue. The best part is that nobody *must* donate, so those who choose not to or can't afford it can still enjoy your content ad-free.

Another method popular on Twitch is the use of **paid subscription options**. This form of earning money is done by essentially encouraging your fans to pay you a recurring fee every month in exchange for a list of benefits. On Twitch, live streamers can offer their subscribers special icons near their name in the chat box, exclusive "emotes" (which are similar to emojis, but custom made by the streamer) to use in chat, as well as a "subscriber only" mode. Live streamers encourage people to subscribe by streaming often and on a regular schedule (people want to know that they're subscribing to an active user, so they can get their money's worth), as well as frequently changing or updating the perks to keep things fun and fresh.

Besides Twitch, owners of blogs or websites can also have a subscription option for their followers. While this is a bit more difficult to set up because it has to be done manually, it can be even more profitable than on Twitch. What you choose to offer your subscribers is ultimately up to you, as well as how much you'll charge them, but it *must* provide value. A lot of people who have a following based on their expertise in a certain area offer courses or programs on their website. A subscription to their course gets you access to the program that will teach you what you're trying to learn, whether its coding, weight loss, cooking, or any other skill you could wish to learn. On top of that, there are usually some "subscriber-only" areas of the website, an exclusive emailed newsletter, and anything else the seller thinks will be of value. This monetization option is a bit more advanced than some of the others and requires a lot of time investment in offering a service worth paying for, so that's something to keep in mind.

A unique way to earn a living off having a large fanbase is by utilizing **affiliate marketing** to promote products. This method can be used effectively by anybody with a large following on any platform and is *really* easy to set up. Essentially, the way this works is you promote a product and provide a special link or URL to the product order page. Anybody who clicks this link and makes a purchase will trigger an affiliate sale for you for the given product. What this means is that you will get a portion of the profits for the sale of the product because you promoted it, similar to the discount code method of sponsorships discussed earlier. While the proceeds from the sale vary greatly depending on the product, most of the time it isn't a *massive* profit. With this method, the idea of scaling up over time is what will gain substantial results, along with gaining a lot of sales, obviously.

There are many sites that offer affiliate programs, most notably Amazon, eBay, ClickBank, Rakuten, and more. All that you need to do is sign up for their affiliate program, choose a product that has an affiliate offer, and have them generate you a special URL that links the product sales page to your affiliate account. From there, it's a matter of encouraging sales and posting your affiliate link to your website, YouTube channel, Instagram bio, and anywhere else it makes sense. Getting people to order using your affiliate link can be accomplished by directly telling people about it, or by using the product or service organically within your content and have the affiliate links to purchase them readily available and displayed prominently.

There are, naturally, many things to consider when taking the affiliate route, some of which has been touched on already for previous monetization methods. First, it's important to **not** promote products that you don't personally think are worth their price tag if you want to remain honest with your fanbase. Again, these people spend time (and sometimes money) supporting you because they enjoy your content, your personality, and because they *trust your judgement*. This recommendation is especially true for some of the questionable information products on ClickBank and other similar digital marketplaces. Secondly, as mentioned before, don't spam your affiliate links or constantly reference them in your content. The most you should do to promote your affiliate links is mention their existence for those interested, and that's it. Finally, it's important to mention again that you should only promote products that make sense for your viewers. If you have a YouTube channel or Instagram page that's centered around beauty products and cosmetics, don't promote a book claiming to teach how you can make money with BitCoin just because that's what's popular at the time. Your viewers won't appreciate the random, irrelevant plug that's a clear attempt at profiting off them.

At this point, hopefully you're beginning to see how lucrative it could be to have a large following online. Additionally, it's worth noting that these are *not* all the ways to make money by having an audience, but they are definitely some of the most common and profitable. Get creative with what you can offer to people who consume your content and try to provide as much value as possible. Keep in mind that successful content creators utilize many of these different monetization methods all at once but found a way to keep it under control, so it doesn't overwhelm their fanbase. Do some trial and error and see which methods you can seamlessly integrate into your content.

- Chapter 6 -
Marketing Materials

Now that we've discussed making content for your desired platform and how you can make money doing it, we need to discuss some things that you should focus on moving forward. Unlike a traditional business that sells goods or services, it's unnecessary to make banners, flyers, or newspaper ads promoting your content. With that being said, there *are* things that you can do to help enhance your online presence so that your growth has less resistance. Essentially, having these things will help to separate you from the amateurs who don't take content creation as serious as you do, and it will make you appear more professional.

The first thing to discuss is something mentioned in chapter 4, which is having a **custom logo and graphics**. To take your content to the next level, it is worth considering having a logo and graphics professionally made for all your social media profiles, your website, your content platforms, and anywhere else online that you have a presence. Now is the time to really think about what kind of unifying themes you want your graphics to have across *all* platforms, this way when followers visit you in various places it all looks how they expect it to. This may not seem like a big deal but knowing what you're going to get from something that you're going to invest time in, for a potential fan, is important. This is much more subliminal than in traditional business, but it can't hurt to implement it to earn points for being professional and consistent. Imagine how weird it would feel going to a McDonalds you've never been to only to be greeted by a giant blue "M" on their sign, and when you walked in, the color scheme was blues and pinks and the employees wore lime green uniforms. While this might not necessarily impact your food or your service, you would certainly question if you were at the right place. The point is, there's a *reason* why every McDonalds looks nearly identical, and it's because it provides a sense of familiarity for customers that we as humans find comforting; we like to know what we're getting. Again, that's an extreme example, but it illustrates why it's beneficial to have your online presence look similar everywhere you post; people like consistency.

Having a uniform appearance online is a major part of **branding**. Branding has been mentioned a few times so far, but now is the time to start considering developing what you want your brand image to be like. If you're not sure where to start on the journey of defining your brand, start by asking yourself what your ultimate mission is for being a content creator. What else, besides earning a living, would you like to accomplish by being a content creator? What benefits and values are you trying to convey to your audience? Defining these things now will help you when you move forward and encounter situations where you will need to make complex decisions.

Staying true to your values and consistently upholding your identity will, again, let viewers know what they're going to get when they see you post new content. Beyond the uniform branding of your message and mission, there comes tying in the imagery and *feel* that you want your content to have. Try thinking of a color scheme, pattern, and recurring elements you would want to have in your graphics. You could have a tropical theme, galaxy theme, city theme, sunshine theme, really the limits are endless. The idea though is that this theme and *feel* will be present in everything you do and across all platforms. This includes everything from the art style of your advertisements to the filters used on Instagram posts. Some may want to take a more modern "minimalist" artistic approach while others might prefer a "rustic" one. If you're having trouble grasping what kind of branding you would want, try thinking about the companies that you like the most. What about their style do you like? Do they have any values that you align with? Besides the branding of the values and appearance, some content creators have a "tagline" or "catch phrase" that they use often. For many, this may be corny or lame, but it could work well for others depending on the demographic of their audience.

Another important piece of marketing material is having your own **website**. Obviously for blog owners this is already established, but for content creators on other platforms a website could still be valuable. One important role that your website will fill is being a place that promotes your entire online presence. Instead of constantly mentioning to your fans that there are other places online where people can follow you, you can instead just plug your website. This will turn multiple links into one, so long as you *do* prominently display them on your homepage. It's also worth noting that you can embed your Instagram and Twitter feeds on your website as well, so people can see all your latest updates in one place.

If you decide to go the route of selling your own merchandise, products, eBooks, or informational courses, the best place to list them is your own website. Assuming you are prepared to fulfill orders all on your own, you can avoid using platforms that will accept orders for you and thus will cut out the middle man. As is typical in any business scenario, if you can eliminate the middle man, your profits tend to be higher. Not only that, but people might be more likely to trust your website when ordering your products than some other site that they've never heard of. Plus, this gives you the chance to handle the customer support experience so that you know that it's the best it can be.

Having your own website is also an additional place that people can find you on the internet. If you post information, updates, content, or blog posts to your website, you can potentially get search engine traffic. By incorporating SEO tactics into your website and your content, you increase your chances of appearing on search results. As mentioned earlier, SEO is the practice of making your website and content easily found by search engines like Google, Yahoo, and Bing when somebody types in a relevant keyword. Besides having your website and content tailored to the keywords that are relevant to what you post, another key to SEO is the number and quality of websites linking back to yours (more on this later). In simple terms, this means that if you embed and link your content on your website, and then link your website in the description of your YouTube video, in your Instagram bio, and so on, then it will overall improve the odds of your content showing up in search results.

Finally, having a website is also another sign of somebody who is professional and takes what they do seriously. It's looks good when you're networking with people to say that they can visit you on your website. Plus, it gives you a place to introduce yourself, tell your story, and give people a place to contact you. Not to mention, having a website is also a great place to further strengthen your brand image!

While I mentioned in chapter 1 not to spread yourself and your energy too thin with creating content for multiple sources all at once, having **social media pages** for your brand is obviously useful. Not only does it provide more places for people to follow you if they want to, it also makes you more visible on the internet.

Typically, posting updates on Facebook or Twitter is easier than creating full content pieces, so it gives you a way to stay better connected with your audience.

Social media is a natural place for fans to ask you questions and interact with you, which is never a bad thing. It's also common for content creators to post on all their social media platforms when they release new content so that the odds of people seeing it are much higher. Plus, if you're stuck and can't think of new content to make, you could also ask those who follow you on social media what they'd like to see, although I wouldn't do this too often. If you're constantly asking for guidance on what to post, your followers will get the impression that you're only making content to please them and not because you enjoy doing it. The last thing you want is for your content to look "forced".

While there exist a nearly-limitless number of materials or methods you could use to promote your content, these are the most fundamental. Having consistent logos, graphics, and branding on your content, website, and social media pages will provide a strong online presence. Establishing this network of interlocked pages will help them feed your content with new and returning viewers. The next thing to master is how to effectively grow on social media itself so that even more people are being funneled to your content.

- Chapter 7 -

Social Media Growth Strategy

The more people discovering you on social media, the more likely they are to click through to your content and become a follower. This is easier said than done though, because social media has become increasingly saturated over the last few years and now it seems everybody is fighting for attention. To break through all the noise, you need to view social media differently than the vast majority of people who use it every single day. Instead of browsing and posting to social media casually whenever you feel like it, there are a few things you can do to make your delivery much more effective.

The first thing you can do to use your social media presence more effectively is to plan your posts by creating a **content calendar**. A content calendar is something commonly used by companies to stay focused on their online presence, and you can easily develop your own as well. Essentially, a content calendar is a way to plan *what* and *when* you're going to post. By planning posts ahead of time, you can more easily incorporate upcoming events, holidays, special releases, and whatever else happens to be going on. On top of that, planning days or weeks ahead will ensure you are posting and updating your social media accounts consistently, even on days when you would normally be too busy to think of anything to post. Additionally, having posts planned will give you time to look it over and make sure that everything you post to all your social media accounts is appropriate for your branding. Of course, if you have a content calendar this doesn't mean you can't still post to Twitter, Facebook, Snapchat, or Instagram as you go about your day, it just means a bulk of the work will have already been done by yourself in advance.

Another thing that a content calendar will help you with is your **post frequency**. This is another key component of growing on social media and is often overlooked. Posting often and staying active on social media is crucial for your page to survive and not fade into obscurity but posting *too* much is also detrimental. Additionally, how often you should post on social media depends on which platform you're using.

Over the last few years, social media sites have changed how they display content so that what is most relevant to your interests will appear first. This is an attempt to please the users of the site; if somebody logs in and is always greeted with posts that are relevant to them, they'll be more likely to continue using the service than if they were always greeted with things they didn't care about. There are a few problems with this approach though, and it isn't always executed as well as some users would like. For example, the algorithms will change over time, so as your interests change, so will the content you see first. This is sometimes inconvenient because it will show content you *are* interested in farther down because of some of the other things you've engaged with recently. Regardless, knowing that this is how social media sites work is key because it will help you understand why you <u>must</u> stay active. If you're inactive for a long period of time, then users will engage with your posts less, which will tell the algorithms that your page isn't as relevant to your followers as much as it used to be, and thus the *next* thing you post will appear farther down on your followers' feeds. As this phenomenon continues to compound, your growth will be stagnant, and you won't get much for your time investment in the platform. However, if you "spam" your followers with posts, a few things could happen. First, your own posts will cannibalize the success of the previous one. This means that your new post will be shown before all your fans had the chance to view you're the one before it, so it gets overshadowed. Secondly, posting tons of times per day to social media is a good way to get your account flagged for spam, which will then tell the platform that your profile has a history of low-quality posts and thus will be less likely to show your new posts to your followers. Therefore, posting frequently is important but finding the sweet spot is key. The amount that you should post on a given platform daily might look something like this:

- Facebook: One or fewer times per day for accounts with less than 10,000 followers, one or two times per day for those with more.

- Twitter: Between three and five tweets per day seems to be a sweet spot for larger brands, but this is less "strict" of a rule than the one for Facebook.

- Instagram: One post per day seems to be perfect, especially because quality over quantity shines true for Instagram. Anything else you'd like to post that day can go on your story, but if you *must* post twice in a single day then that's perfectly fine too.

- Snapchat: One to five posts per day to your story should be enough to remain consistent, although Snapchat operates differently than the other social media sites on this list. Skipping a day should be okay on Snapchat if you don't have anything interesting to post.

- <u>Pinterest:</u> One to three pins per day seems to be optimal. This network isn't needed for many content creators, but some niches can thrive here.

Obviously, these are just general recommendations and it's always best to do some testing yourself. What might work for one person in a certain industry might not work for another because their demographics might use social media differently. Always view your analytics and see what works and what doesn't when it comes to post frequency.

Another thing that is related strongly to your consistency and post frequency is your **post time**. The time that you post either new content or new updates to social media matters tremendously, more so than most people realize. It's important to understand the primary demographic of your audience and what they do on a day-to-day basis, as well as what time it is where they are. Consider where you live when posting, but also consider where your primary demographic lives as well because different time zones will mean different post times. If, for example, you live in New York and a decent amount of your audience is in California, posting your content at 1 P.M. will likely get less engagement because that's equivalent to 11 A.M. in California; a time where many people are already at work or school in *both* time zones. It would be better to try to post when most of your demographic is free such as before work, after school, or during lunch hours. Luckily, analytics on most platforms will tell you where your audience is primarily located, so use that information to your advantage. Finding the sweet spot for when you should post on social media takes some trial and error, but it will make a big difference.

Since it's difficult to be active on social media at the same time every single day, having a way to schedule your posts is crucial. This will allow you to create a post in advance and have it post automatically later. The primary way to accomplish this, as well as provide you with some other valuable perks, is by using a **social media dashboard**. These websites allow you to manage many of your social media accounts all in one convenient place, effectively removing the need to remember to go to all of them individually.

Additionally, most of them allow you to schedule posts depending on which social media site you're making content for. As another added benefit, social media dashboards usually give you multiple analytics for the data that's collected from all your social media accounts since they're all linked to one place. This will give you better insight into what to post where, when to post on different sites, and so on. There are a lot of social media dashboards out there, but some of the biggest are HootSuite, SproutSocial, Falcon, and ZoHo.

Finally, one of the most crucial pieces to any social media strategy is **engagement**. By this I don't mean getting lots of engagement from your followers (which is *always* a good thing), I mean engaging with your followers yourself! After all, the whole point of social media is being social. Not only does evidence suggest that actively engaging with your audience boosts the rankings of your posts, but it has a compounding effect. If your followers know that you'll respond to them, they're more likely to leave a comment. Additionally, the more comments you get, the more engagement you receive, and thus it becomes a self-fulfilling cycle. By engaging with your followers, you also build a better relationship with them which will make them more loyal to you overall. Not only that, but from a business perspective, loyal fans are more likely to buy your merchandise or products you recommend, which is a plus. Your followers *want* to be heard and they *want* to interact with you. If you're just starting out, this is a **huge** advantage you have over people with bigger audiences because they have too many followers to respond to them all, plus they probably have less time to read and respond to comments.

By now, you should be beginning to understand the fundamentals of building your following on social media. To summarize, the most important key parts of growing on social media are:

- Plan what you're going to post
- Be consistent and post often
- Post at optimal times to maximize exposure
- Use a dashboard to make your life easier
- Engage with your followers

If you do these 5 things while posting quality content, long-term success on social media is guaranteed. Remember, analytics will guide you along the way so you can change, adapt, and improve what you're doing and continue to grow.

- Chapter 8 -

Effective Online Presence

While having an effective social media presence is invaluable, knowing how to stand out on the internet in general is an important skill to have. Besides, posting consistently to social media might mean little to nothing if very few people can even find you. A few years ago, when fewer competitors were fighting for the attention of your audience, getting discovered wasn't *that* hard. Nowadays, it's important to use every trick of the trade to increase your odds of being found online because that could be the difference between having a career and not.

The first tool that you should master when developing your online presence is how to pick and use **keywords**. This goes back to what was discussed in both Chapter 4 and Chapter 6 about SEO but needs to be reiterated here. Keyword optimization doesn't have to be limited to websites or blog posts, keywords can be effectively used for any type of content being created. Using the right keywords when posting on social media, writing the description of your YouTube videos, and when building your website, will give you good practice when it comes to learning how to optimize content for search engines. If you're going to post *anything* to *any* platform, you might as well incorporate keywords to improve the content's visibility.

When trying to pick keywords, there are many tools available to use. The most basic one and the easiest to use is Google Trends. By going to Google Trends, you can compare two or more words or phrases to see which are searched more often. This is especially useful when you're trying to figure out the title of a YouTube video or Blog post. While the data offered is relatively limited, it does show search volume over a set period, plus it will give you geographic data as well as related searches. The second most basic tool you can use is Google Ads' Keyword Planner. This is another free service that can be obtained by having a Google Ads account, and it will help you pick different keywords based on one that you've suggested. Not only does it show you how often the keywords are searched, but it also shows how much competition each keyword has. What's important to know is that you want to target keywords that have high search volume but low competition, although this is almost always easier said than done. Picking the right set of keywords for each post is both a science *and* an art, so practice really is the best way to get it right. Starting this practice early will give you a *massive* edge against your competition, especially because many people don't fully understand SEO.

Another major trick to have in your arsenal is the use of **Power Words**. If keywords are what get search engines to display your content, power words are what get people to click on it. These words are more of a psychological trigger that causes the reader to be influenced into clicking the content. Often, power words are what make "clickbait" so enticing, even if you know that the title of the content is probably just an exaggeration. Power words are essentially words or phrases that, when used in almost any context, get people's attention because it aligns with human nature. Power words are effective because they can be used to persuade people to act by having a subconscious emotional response to them. Additionally, using power words in the form a question is even more powerful, but let's use some examples to really illustrate how power words work. Which of these two titles to a YouTube video would you be more likely to click on?

"Top Weight Loss Tips for Women!"
-or-
"6 Ridiculously Simple Ways to Lose 5 Pounds in Less than 2 Weeks!"

Most people would find the second title more appealing, for a few reasons. The first reason is the use of the power words, which in this case are "Ridiculously", "Simple", and "in Less than". These words are exaggerated words that cause the reader to feel a certain type of way about whatever the subject of the title is, in this case weight loss. The second thing that makes the second title more enticing is that it's specific. It gives a specific number of ways to lose weight, how much weight they can lose, as well as a time frame for which it will work. Additionally, the time frame is relatively short which is attractive for readers.

Power words work by subconsciously playing with some of human's most powerful emotions and desires, and usually fall into one of the following categories:

- Greed
- Fear
- Curiosity
- Anger
- Sloth
- Trust
- Lust
- Vanity

The Greed power words play on the natural human tendency to want to acquire more than we really need. These words relate often to scarcity or how easy it is to obtain something. (Ex. "Watch our FREE training session on how to lose weight fast!")

The Fear power words influence human's primitive instinct to avoid things that could harm them. These words will suggest something bad could happen if the reader doesn't act. (Ex. "Don't make the mistake of missing out on our latest posts!")

Curiosity power words cause a mental "itch" that we naturally want to scratch, and that is only accomplished by getting the answer to something we're told we don't know. (Ex. "Could this shocking secret cause you to lose subscribers?")

Anger power words are meant to subconsciously stir up irrational anger to influence decision making. This can either be aimed at a common enemy or could be used to preface a solution. (Ex. "Are you sick and tired of wasting time and money on the latest fad diet? Try THIS instead!")

The Sloth power words influence our natural desire to avoid hard work while still achieving results. These words suggest that even if you're lazy, you can still obtain what you want. (Ex. "This effortless trick to building a profitable website will make you money on demand!")

Trust power words are used to subliminally build up trust between you, the content creator, and the visitor who is reading what you have to say. (Ex. "Studies show that this ONE trick is guaranteed to improve your search engine rankings, no questions asked!")

Lust power words are used to increase a person's desire or craving for something. Usually, if somebody is craving something they will act less rationally to get it, or in other words, click on your content to satisfy that feeling of lust. (Ex. "Everybody is obsessing over this mind-blowing new video game!")

Vanity power words encourage action because it uses our innate drive to appear better either to ourselves or to others. People naturally want to look and feel successful, so playing on that fact usually gets results. (Ex. "This remarkable formula will have staggering effects on the growth of your business!")

Obviously, the examples used in this section were exaggerated a bit to get the point across. Your claims and content titles don't want to sound as "sales pitchy" as the examples used here, but the concept holds true. By rewording the titles of your content, you can strongly encourage people to click on it and at least see what you have to say. This may even be the one thing that's been preventing your content from growing in the first place, so don't underestimate the effectiveness of including power words.

A list of over 575 of the most influential power words has been included for free at the very end of this book, so don't forget to reference them as your post more content!

While this may not be necessary for everybody, paying for **online advertisement campaigns** may be valuable for some niches. While it often doesn't make sense to pay for ads that simply ask for people to view a regular piece of your content, they *could* be used to push products, courses, or whatever else you may be selling. Additionally, when you've grown your community to large sizes, online ads can push the boundaries of organic traffic and can be used to increase brand awareness. Targeted ads could be used to help promote events you're hosting, giveaways, and much more. The more creative you can get with paid ads as a content creator, the better. Again, this is *not* a shortcut to gaining viewers and fans, because typically low levels of engagement are involved when somebody is paid to see an ad, but it can help later down the line for a many different aspects of running an online business. With that being said, it's important to at least learn the basics of paid ads at some point, which is what is going to be discussed here. The two main platforms that people use are Facebook (which also owns Instagram) as well as Google.

As of 2018, Facebook has over 2 billion *active* users, a status given to users that have logged into the platform at least once within the last 30 days. This means that by using Facebook ads, you can tap into over 25% of the entire world's population. Thankfully, Facebook allows you to target specific demographics with a variety of targeting options:

- Location: This reaches potential customers based on where they live, and can target based on country, state/province, city, area code, or zip code.

- <u>Demographic:</u> Lets you reach people based on age, gender, relationship, education, level, job title, and much more.
- <u>Lookalike:</u> Allows you to reach prospects that are similar to your current customers, fans, or website visitors.
- <u>Behaviors:</u> Allows you to reach customers based on their actions, such as what device they're logging in from, what content they like, and more.
- <u>Interests:</u> Allows you to reach people based on what they enjoy, their hobbies, what pages they like on Facebook, and more.
- <u>Website Custom Audiences:</u> Attempts to reach people who have already visited your website before and ended up leaving. This can be customized to include people who visited a product page, people who put something in their "Shopping Cart" but didn't purchase, and so on. This requires the use of the Facebook Pixel code which needs to be put onto your website to relay data back to Facebook.

As a side note, if you've just started your content creation journey and you're struggling to get your first few fans, Facebook friends are a great way to start. First, build a sufficiently decent Facebook fan page for your content. Next, invite some of your friends that you think may like your content. With any luck, a few of them will "Like" your page, enjoy what you're doing, and that will be your humble beginnings!

Another interesting thing that Facebook offers is the ability to "Boost" your posts. This could be useful if you already have a solid following on Facebook but haven't been active in a while. When you create a piece of content that you don't want your Facebook audience to miss, boosting a post that features your content could be a cheap and effective way to make sure people see it.

As of 2018, Google sees over 100 billion searches per month, which is equivalent to 40,000 searches per second. Over 3 billion people use Google every month around the world, and 75% of people who use search engines choose Google. Again, these staggering numbers mean very little unless you can target specific users that would be interested in your content, and thankfully Google provides many tools to do so:

- Location: Allows targeting by country, region, city, and more but it also can access user's exact location if they're on a mobile device or newer computer. This means that you can target people within a few miles of a specific location that may be relevant to you.
- Demographic: Allows targeting of people based on gender, age, parental status, marital status, and so on. On top of that, it also allows language targeting to focus based on language preferences.
- Keyword: Targets people who are searching for a specific word or phrase. This is perfect for blog posts that you want to promote to a broader audience. Additionally, Negative keyword targeting allows you to exclude yourself from reaching people who are searching for a specific word or phrase. This further increases the accuracy of your chose audience.
- Device: Lets you reach people who use a specific device or device type, such as a computer, mobile device, or tablet.

While it was mentioned earlier that Instagram was owned by Facebook, it's still worth noting some of the key differences between paying to advertise on each platform. Instagram alone has almost 1 billion monthly active users, with over 500 million of them logging on every single day. Over 4 billion likes are performed on Instagram per day, and over 100 million photos are uploaded to the platform daily. When choosing to advertise on Instagram, you can pick a goal to strive for, either more profile visits, more website traffic, or simply more people viewing your ad. Targeting can also be done just like on Facebook, but it's a little more limited on Instagram. Targeting can include user location, interests, age, and gender.

One common way people like to compare the two mega platforms, Facebook and Google, is by suggesting Google ads are best for getting immediate results whereas Facebook and Instagram ads are best for increasing brand awareness and generating leads for sales. This makes sense when taking into consideration how each of these platforms work. People search for things on Google because they are looking for a solution in that very moment, or in other words, they are in a state of "actively searching". There's a good chance that if the ad that appears at the top of their search results is exactly what they were looking for, then they will buy it on the spot because it's what they were looking for to begin with. However, with Facebook and Instagram, users are browsing more passively, either to kill time or in search of entertainment. People who see ads while in the "passively browsing" state aren't actually looking to buy anything. These people can still be influenced to buy, but it's more likely that they will pay attention to ads that are simply increasing brand awareness or giving something out for free in exchange for contact information. This is not to say that Google Ads should ONLY be used to get immediate sales and that Facebook Ads should ONLY be used to increase brand awareness and generate leads, but based on how people generally use the platforms, this is usually the case.

It's important to stress that spending hundreds of dollars advertising your content when you're a beginner is *not* a good idea. The return on this investment will likely be unsustainable and will discourage you from continuing to pursue your goals. Use online advertisements sparingly and only when you have some extra money to invest. As mentioned before, these ads are most useful to promote special occasions revolving around your content creation brand, promotions you may be involved in or running, milestones in your career, or sales you might be having on related product launches (if you ever go that route). Once you have a sustainable income from content creation, you know that it will be a stable job for you, and that you love to do it, you can dabble in using these ads to increase brand awareness and reach farther than your organic traffic sources would typically allow.

Once you've gotten the hang of being a content creator and you have the time and energy to spare, it's worth looking into **expanding to new platforms**. Whether you have a blog, a YouTube channel, a weekly gaming live stream, or you're an influencer on social media, there is something else you could be doing on another platform to enhance both your business and your online presence. This section will discuss what content you could be creating on *other* platforms in conjunction with your primary platform you chose in chapters 1 and 4.

If you chose to focus on being a YouTuber, expanding to other platforms is relatively straightforward. Having an Instagram account for your channel could come in handy for many different reasons. For one, it could be a place where you "pull back the curtain" and show your true fans what you daily life is like. This would involve posting pictures and videos of things you do and places you go. Gamers can post short gameplay clips, beauty vloggers can post their outfits, cooking channels can post their food, musicians can post their lifestyle, and the list goes on.

Depending on what your content is, live streaming can also be a natural extension of your content. For gamers, this is a no-brainer, but for others it could get a bit tricky to see the fruits of your labor investing the time and effort into live streaming. Many online personalities do "IRL" streams on Twitch or YouTube (which stands for "In Real Life") where they sit in front of a camera for a few hours conversing with their audience in real time, listening to music, and discussing various topics. This could work for many people too, but it's tricky for certain niches.

A blog could also be a natural extension of a YouTube channel, depending on the content. Having a blog with information that supplements your videos could be a great way to give your viewers more information that you simply can't fit into a video. Plus, it's much easier to go back and edit a blog post with updates than it is to take down a video, add content, and re-upload it. A blog works great for cooking channels, where they can post recipes, fitness channels, where they can post tips and workout plans, and really any other channel that falls into the "how to" or "educational" category. What's even better is that embedding your YouTube video into your blog post will likely help the search rankings of both pieces of content!

Creating content for Facebook can be useful for a YouTuber as well, and there are many different approaches that can be taken. For instance, YouTubers who tend to post long videos will break up the video into smaller bits that are more easily consumed and post them on Facebook. Some notable YouTubers who have done this very well in the past are Philip DeFranco and Gary Vaynerchuk, just to name a couple. If that isn't the case with your content, you could always post different video content that might be shorter and less professional, but is funnier, more personal, or quirkier. If that isn't your style, then perhaps status updates to connect with your audience or high-quality photos that relate to your niche, daily life, and so on.

If you chose to be an <u>Instagram influencer</u>, the good news is that spreading to other platforms is not only common, but basically expected. Since it's not possible to run ads on Instagram *directly* through the platform itself, having a YouTube channel is a great way to monetize your follower base. Since Instagram only allows for a peek into your day to day life, YouTube can be a way to really engage with your followers and provide them with even more of the content you've been posting on Instagram.

As with certain niches within YouTube, live streaming on Twitch and other services only makes sense for some Instagram influencers. While you could always go the "IRL" stream route, this might not make sense for everybody. If you want to get into live streaming as an Instagram influencer, you may need to carve out a slightly different niche first. Otherwise, you could use live streams for special events like Question and Answer sessions (Q&A's) or special guests.

Having a blog as an Instagram user can also be a great way to monetize your fanbase by providing more content than Instagram itself allows. As mentioned above when discussing Instagram influencers on YouTube, Instagram itself doesn't really allow for long, in-depth content. With that being said, having a blog can be your outlet for that sort of content, and naturally, can feature your photography skills as well.

Finally, having a Facebook fan page for an Instagram influencer may not make much sense unless it's being used to live stream or promote your blog. Content that works well on Facebook also works somewhat well on Instagram too, so having both doesn't really make sense unless you've grown to a massive size and start to push mini-celebrity status. Of course, having a Facebook fan page can be useful to reach your broad audience, but until then, it might not make sense.

If you originally chose to focus on <u>Twitch or live streaming</u> in general, moving to something like YouTube is fairly straightforward. In many instances, people who live stream will upload either parts of their stream, or their stream as a whole, to YouTube. This is particularly easy if you live stream on YouTube itself, and is a good idea because it allows people to enjoy your streams after the fact. This works particularly well for people who live stream video game content, which is the majority of Twitch, but also can work for other types of live stream content as well.

As with previous platforms, expanding to Instagram for a Twitch streamer is pretty straightforward and could be a way to engage more closely with your audience when you aren't available to go live. Additionally, Instagram itself has a live stream feature that can be used on the go, so if you're traveling or too busy for a dedicated stream, a mobile live stream could be quick and fun for your audience. Remember, people are often fascinated by the lives of those who do what they love for a living, so use this to your advantage when posting on Instagram. Let others see your daily life and what it looks like, especially if you're doing exciting things!

Having a blog as a live streamer may not be as useful as it was for the previous two content creator choices. Since live streaming tends to involve long pieces of video content, there likely won't be much information left over for a blog. Also, the demographic you're likely pulling in as a live streamer probably aren't people who like to read pages of text. Unlike YouTubers, there aren't as many live streamers who are "education" or "how-to" oriented because of the nature of live streaming itself, and thus, it's difficult to adapt live stream content into blog articles. While it certainly is possible to have a blog alongside a live stream channel, there are probably better uses of your time.

Finally, having a Facebook fan page for your live stream content could be useful, but would require some planning and creativity. Similar to YouTube, clips and portions of a full live stream can be uploaded to Facebook in order to reach that audience. These clips should be ones that are most likely to be shared or "go viral", because as it stands, people don't necessarily turn to Facebook for lengthy video content. As with everything previously mentioned, Facebook is also a great place for engagement with your fans while you're offline.

Having chosen to have your own Blog, expanding to new platforms is both natural and very effective. As the inverse of what was discussed for YouTube content creators, starting a YouTube channel after growing your Blog is a great way to get more visitors to your site, as well as a good way to improve the quality of your posts. As mentioned before, your YouTube channel can offer supplemental content to your Blog or vice versa. Some things are easier shown than written about, so having a YouTube channel to get those points across can be incredibly valuable as well.

Creating content for an Instagram profile to supplement your blog posts could be incredibly useful if you have the time and resources to dedicate to growing it. This works especially well for niches like cooking, fitness, or modern entrepreneurship, but some others might struggle. Anything you can teach or write about on a blog could also be shown off on Instagram and having both is a great way to cross-promote your content. Telling your story through images is what makes an Instagram account successful, so striving to do that with any niche is the key.

As mentioned before, live streaming and blogs don't *typically* go hand-in-hand, so having a Twitch account to supplement your blog isn't really necessary. If your blog surrounds video games, then naturally Twitch would be perfect, but otherwise Facebook or YouTube might be the better place for live streaming.

Facebook is great for bloggers because it's a surefire way to at *least* get your content in front of your own personal audience. Not only that, but getting a following on Facebook also allows you to push your content in front of your audience when they aren't even visiting your site. Now, of course, spamming is *never* a good idea, but regularly posting about your latest posts or maybe one from a while back that you feel is high quality is definitely welcome. Not only that, but you can (as mentioned) use Facebook to live stream certain events like Q&A's, interviews, and whatever else you're able to come up with.

As mentioned in chapter 4, most large and successful Facebook pages are general hobby or niche pages. With that being said, if you've successfully grown a Facebook page all on its own, venturing out into other platforms for content creation could prove challenging. Most likely, the content you've posted to Facebook on a daily basis is what gets people engaged in the first place, and since (most of the time) large Facebook pages aren't person-specific, that content is really all people want to see from that page. If you begin interjecting plugs for your new blog, YouTube channel, or Twitch stream, people will likely be less receptive. That doesn't mean that it's impossible though!

Having a YouTube channel that piggybacks off of your Facebook page could work for some niches like fitness or cooking, two niches that have been referenced a lot so far! Typically, people will start on YouTube and move to Facebook after but doing it the other way around could work too.

An Instagram page that supports a Facebook page might be a bit repetitive, primarily because the content posted to both is rather similar. However, photographers and artists might be able to pull both off simultaneously. Interestingly enough, "meme pages" could probably do this the best, as can be seen by people like "f*ckjerry".

There aren't many instances where a Facebook page will smoothly be able to transition to Twitch, especially since you'll likely get more viewers of your live content if you simply choose to go live on Facebook instead. Again, Twitch and gaming go flawlessly, so if that's your niche then it is viable, but otherwise there's little reason to fight an uphill battle attempting to transition from Facebook to Twitch. On top of this, Facebook has recently been trying to increase the number of gamers streaming on their platform, so if that's your niche, it still may make more sense to stick to Facebook.

Finally, having a blog support your Facebook following is useful, but also a bit backwards. Typically, content creators start a blog and spread with Facebook, not the other way around, but that doesn't mean that you shouldn't try if you already have the Facebook following to go with it. Making a website and a blog that will supply your Facebook audience with quality, useful content is something that will likely appreciate it if the niche is ripe for it.

It's worth noting that there are other areas to expand into besides just the ones listed here. Many content creators, upon getting large enough followings, branch out and do other things like write books, dabble in acting, or start podcasts. As mentioned at the very beginning of this book, content creation is all about *passion* so whatever you're passionate about can be something you can make part of your career. Don't limit what you do!

If you want to get into app development, software engineering, or starting a totally different business, those are all perfectly good routes to take. It goes without saying that if you're going to branch out in this way, make sure you have a solid game plan and have the resources necessary to make it work.

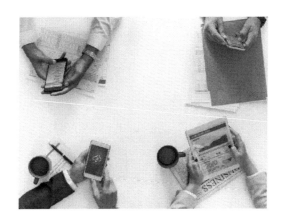

- Chapter 9 -

Networking and Collaboration

The saying "If you want to go far, go together" couldn't be truer for growing a following online. In the earlier days of the internet, content creators didn't have nearly as much competition as they do now, so this was less important (although still done extensively). Regardless of the platform, the idea is that by teaming up with somebody else and cross-promoting each other's content, you effectively both double your exposure; all of their followers who may have never heard of you otherwise are now getting exposed to what you do. Beyond that, simply networking with others in your space is a good way to get your name out there and become better known by your peers.

For YouTubers, collaborating goes way back to the beginning of the site. The concept is simple and comes in many different forms. In its most basic form, collaborating with another YouTuber simply involves you both making two videos together; one for your channel and one for theirs. Naturally, you'll both want to upload these videos around the same time and should link each other's profile in the description of the video. Collaborations work with pretty much any niche so long as you both can come up with creative ideas for videos. For channels that provide commentary, you could simply get on a skype call and record a conversation about a particular topic. For vloggers and other niches, you may need to be in person with the other content creator, but this opens the door to more possibilities. Cooking channels can share their favorite recipes, vloggers can visit new cities, fitness channels can share their favorite workouts, and gamers can play together. In some instances, the trend on YouTube was to start drama with another channel as a way to promote one another. For many, this tactic was incredibly useful, but for some it ruined their channel, so proceed with caution! Also, many people can see through fake drama and they may lose respect for you as a result.

Instagram collaborations work in a more basic way. While you could post on each other's accounts, it's more common to either post pictures with each other or shout out one another's accounts using Instagram's story feature. This is true of Facebook too, but primarily done by sharing a post from each other's page and tagging the post creator. In both instances it's important to actually tell your audience to go follow the person you're collaborating with!

Collaborating on Twitch is relatively straightforward. Typically, streamers will play in the same games together with voice chat turned on so the audience can hear both content creators, or they'll get into a skype call with one another. Additionally, what some creators will do is "Host" the person that they're working with. Hosting is a feature that Twitch offers where you can put somebody else's live stream on your Twitch channel, so all of your followers will see their stream. This can be set up to be done automatically when you're offline. This means that if you're not streaming but the person you're working with is, then their content will be automatically hosted on your channel as well until you turn the Host feature off.

Collaborating for bloggers is also incredibly common and is one of the best ways to reach a new audience. Typically, when two bloggers collaborate, they do what is called "**guest posting**". This means that they each write an article or blog post for the other person's blog, with author credit going to them and a plug for their own website. This is beneficial for multiple reasons, the most obvious one being that your content gets seen by a whole new audience. Besides that, the link from their website to yours is what is called a "backlink". Essentially, a backlink is a connection between one website to yours. In other words, any time your URL is posted to a new website, it creates a new backlink. This is important because backlinks are a piece of the search engine formula. The theory is that the more websites linking back to yours, the more valuable and credible your site must be. However, this *does not* mean that you can simply post your link everywhere and you will suddenly shoot to the number one spot on google search rankings. Each backlink has a quality ranking, meaning that a backlink from a highly reputable website will be more valuable than one from a website that's barely visited. The reason for this was because in the past, internet marketers would actually purchase backlinks from people who had a computer generate thousands of websites *solely* for the purpose of making backlinks. These websites made in bulk would have generic blocks of jumbled text, usually just lists of keywords, and somewhere on the page would be the links people paid to have listed. This led to a lot of low-quality websites getting promoted by Google's search algorithm, and it led to a bad experience for people searching for things on the platform. Nowadays, purchasing low quality backlinks in bulk is still possible, but it may actually result in your website getting a *worse* search ranking. This punishment by Google and other search engines is a way to deter people from trying to game the system, so it's generally advised not to go that route.

While malicious attempts to artificially boost the rankings of your site in search results are being monitored, it is still very beneficial to have legitimate backlinks to your website. This is where guest posting shines, but you can also create your own backlinks. For instance, posting a link to an article you wrote on Reddit will count as a backlink. Get creative with where you share your content, and if it's relevant and well received, it may be a strong backlink!

The last thing to mention with regards to networking and collaborating is attending events where networking opportunities are abundant. No matter what platform or niche you create content for, there is likely some sort of event or convention in a major city near you that will be an excellent place to meet others in your industry. Both VidCon for YouTubers and TwitchCon for Twitch streamers come to mind immediately, but there are plenty of other smaller events in cities all around the world. If you can, attend these events as often as possible and try to meet new people. Being able to reach out to people of different talents, backgrounds, and social circles is crucial for a successful entertainer.

Everybody has heard of the "six degrees of separation" rule, which essentially suggests that you are at most 6 connections away from any person on the planet. In essence, somebody you know may also know somebody who knows somebody who knows somebody you want to connect with. With the rise of social media, this famous rule has actually *decreased to four*. This means that you are at most 4 connections away from any famous actor or actress. Understanding the magnitude of this statistic means that the more people you work with, the number of potential followers of your content goes up *exponentially*. This means that, given the opportunity, you should attend as many things you are invited to as possible. Even if it is a group of friends getting together for dinner, maybe somebody brings a friend or significant other that you haven't met yet. Additionally, as mentioned before, there are usually large networking events in a city near you and they are often times free. As a small side note, if you're in college, you *automatically* have access to dozens of free clubs and events that happen every week! Regardless, no matter the event, there are a few tips for networking that can improve your odds at making meaningful connections:

- Arrive Early: You may think it's a better use of your time to arrive a little late so that there are a lot more people there when you get there, but the quality of your interactions is more important than the quantity. By arriving early, there will be fewer people there and approaching individuals is much easier than trying to get into a group of people already engaged in conversation.

- <u>Ask Questions:</u> People love talking about themselves, so make them feel special by asking questions about themselves, what they do, and their content in general. Starting off small with questions like "What brings you this event?" are a good way to start a conversation. The most important part about this tip is to actually listen to what they say. Use their responses to fuel your conversation and try to remember what they say.

- <u>Don't Be A Salesman:</u> Resist the urge to start pitching your content to everybody you meet. The idea of a networking event is to get to know people, not to get everybody to follow you on social media. Building a relationship with somebody is much more valuable in the long run, and people are much more likely to do business with people they know and like. If somebody *does* ask about what you do, give them a simple overview, and maybe include some milestones or accomplishments that have happened lately.

- <u>Share Passionate Stories:</u> Be prepared to tell a good story about why you started making content. Most people have a boring and mundane day-to-day life, so being passionate and exciting sets you apart.

People want to be around those who are passionate because it's a breath of fresh air for them. It's always good to hear about people who love what they do!

- Give More Then You Take: This is a good rule for life, but it applies here too. Don't dominate a conversation talking about yourself or your content. Be somebody who likes having a good conversation, not somebody who just likes to talk. Make others feel important or special so that they like you.

- Be Open and Smile: Your body language says a lot about you before you even open your mouth. If you're hunched over with your arms crossed and a bored look on your face, people will assume that you're not having a good time. When was the last time somebody who was having a bad time made you feel good? Probably never, so don't give somebody a reason not to talk to you. Make sure to smile, be inviting, and give a solid handshake.

- Follow Up: If you have a good interaction with somebody, don't forget to get their contact information before you leave. While the event itself may be fun, it is the beginning of a friendship, not an end in itself. Make sure to follow up with people within a day or two so that they know you're interested in keeping in touch.

With these tips, having meaningful interactions shouldn't be too much of an issue. As a final note regarding networking and collaborations, make sure to keep an open mind. You may be shy or thinking that a collaboration won't help you, but it could help in ways you may never have anticipated. One thing people don't realize when they're in the habit of creating content is that they may be missing out on a new way of doing things. Collaborating with others is a great way to revitalize your creativity and get inspired to continue doing what you love.

Closing Thoughts

The world of content creation is one that is ever-changing and will force you to find creative and innovative ways to adapt in order to grow and maintain an engaged audience. Despite the vast differences in creating content for all of the varying platforms, niches, and demographics, hopefully this book was able to distill it all down to a few key concepts that you may not have fully known or understood before. Armed with the knowledge in this book, you will be better equipped than a vast majority of the content creators in your niche, but that doesn't mean success is guaranteed. Aim for long-term success when it comes to growing an audience, and always keep your primary goals in mind. Continue to ask yourself why you want to be a content creator, and remind yourself when you feel you've gotten to a point where you can hardly remember. If pushing out content begins to feel like an unfulfilling grind, remember why you started. Realize the impact that you can have on your audience and the world around you when you have a fan base who listens to you, trusts you, and will hear your message. Use your amplified voice to spread messages of positivity and kindness, and do your best to avoid the negatives that can come along with this career. Last but not least, if your content ever gets popular enough to where you begin to make serious money off of it, always keep your mental health in check. Many YouTubers, musicians, models, streamers, and others in the entertainment business often feel their mental health degrade when all eyes are on them.

I would also like to take a moment to thank you, the reader, for supporting this book. This book is the first one I've ever written, edited, and published all on my own! It took many hours of planning, research, and formatting, so I hope it helps you in some way.

As a final note, it's worth mentioning that since the world of content creation is always evolving, I continuously post new articles, tips, and strategies for growing and marketing an online business on my website. You can sign up for consultation services as well if you'd like me to take a personal look at your business! I've worked with businesses of all sizes and the first session is free just so I can get to know you!

www.greystonestrategy.com

For additional free content, don't forget to subscribe to Greystone Strategy on YouTube as well! Follow us on social media so you know exactly when we post new content!

YouTube:
https://www.youtube.com/channel/UCF4xNvTkDlLKu8PJQZo61JA

Instagram:
https://www.instagram.com/greystonestrategy

Facebook:
https://www.facebook.com/GreystoneStrategy/

Twitter:
https://twitter.com/GreystoneStrat

Power Words

As discussed in Chapter 8, the following is an extensive list of over 575 of the most influential power words! The list is broken up by emotion so it's easier to find what you're looking for.

Greed:

1. Frugal
2. Guilt-free
3. Discount
4. While they last
5. Triple
6. Sale ends soon
7. Profit
8. Jackpot
9. Before
10. Soaring
11. More
12. Whopping
13. Cash
14. New
15. Bargain
16. Prize
17. Best
18. Rich
19. First
20. Surge
21. Ultimate
22. Pay zero
23. Economical
24. Big
25. Massive
26. Expires
27. Reduced
28. Luxurious
29. Up-sell
30. Limited
31. Premiere Price break
32. Deadline
33. Value
34. Monetize
35. Bonus
36. Billion
37. Cheap
38. Last chance
39. Final
40. Gift
41. Extra
42. Now
43. Six-figure
44. Bonanza
45. Quick
46. Money
47. Never again
48. Dollar
49. Treasure
50. Double
51. Running out
52. Skyrocket
53. Savings
54. Explode
55. Don't miss out
56. Greatest
57. Save
58. Giveaway
59. Exclusive
60. Fast
61. Special
62. Marked down
63. Instantly
64. Hurry
65. Fortune
66. Frenzy
67. Feast
68. Quadruple
69. Inexpensive

Fear:

1. Savage
2. Bloody
3. Drowning
4. Frightening
5. Death
6. Crisis
7. Slave
8. Wreaking havoc
9. Cripple
10. Devastating
11. Cataclysmic
12. Pale
13. Strangle
14. Mistake
15. Lawsuit
16. Painful
17. Feeble
18. Trauma
19. Horrific
20. Beating
21. IRS
22. Reckoning
23. Backlash
24. Buffoon
25. Toxic
26. Scary
27. Corpse
28. Revenge
29. Danger
30. Lunatic
31. Bumbling
32. Warning
33. Hack
34. Hazardous
35. Scream
36. Crazy
37. Teetering
38. Poison
39. Collapse
40. Caution
41. Murder
42. Dangerous
43. Trap
44. Torture
45. Insidious
46. Frantic
47. Silly
48. Terror
49. Volatile
50. Fired Fool
51. Plunge
52. Embarrass
53. Cadaver
54. Shatter
55. Suffering
56. Stupid
57. Epidemic
58. Peril
59. Tank
60. Pus
61. Suck
62. Plague
63. Risky
64. Smash
65. Deadly
66. Catastrophe
67. Vulnerable
68. Hurricane
69. Played
70. Beware

71. Wounded
72. Assault
73. Poor
74. Prison
75. Pummel
76. Piranha
77. Slaughter
78. Nightmare
79. Worry
80. Searing
81. Bomb
82. Meltdown
83. Pitfall
84. Plummet
85. Terrorist
86. Invasion
87. Panic
88. Tailspin
89. Victim
90. Gullible
91. Jail
92. Dumb
93. Disastrous
94. Bloodcurdling
95. Armageddon
96. Annihilate
97. Targeted
98. Lurking
99. Shellacking
100. Gambling
101. Blood
102. Jeopardy
103. Destroy
104. Bloodbath
105. Looming
106. Blinded
107. Mired

108. Hoax
109. Fooled
110. Fail
111. Agony
112. Refugee
113. Vaporize
114. Tragedy
115. Apocalypse

Curiosity:

1. Privy
2. Hilarious
3. Hush-hush
4. Dark
5. Controversial
6. Spoiler
7. Shh!
8. Shocking
9. Psycho
10. Sneak peak
11. Under wraps
12. Unbelievable
13. Concealed
14. Insane
15. Members only
16. Behind the scenes
17. Outlawed
18. Wacky
19. Banned
20. Key
21. Untold
22. Uncharted
23. Zany
24. Forgotten
25. Strange
26. Unauthorized

27. Forbidden
28. Unexplained
29. Top secret
30. Astonishing
31. Cover-up
32. Eye-opening
33. Ridiculous
34. Undiscovered
35. Lost
36. Insider
37. Illegal
38. Underground
39. Secret
40. Trade secret
41. Black market
42. Unheard of
43. Login required
44. Class full
45. On the quiet
46. Bootleg
47. Unusual
48. Covert
49. Extraordinary
50. Interesting
51. Censored
52. Be the first
53. Backdoor
54. Odd
55. Myths
56. Closet
57. Unconventional
58. Invitation only
59. Unlock
60. Smuggled
61. Elusive
62. Off the record
63. Blacklisted
64. Priceless
65. Stunning
66. Crazy
67. Incredibly
68. Under the table
69. Secrets
70. Unexplored
71. Cringeworthy
72. Hidden
73. Private
74. Restricted
75. Off-limits
76. Illusive
77. Thought-provoking
78. Super Secret
79. Little-known
80. Withheld
81. Unique
82. Remote
83. Bizarre
84. Classified
85. Confessions
86. Become an insider
87. Confidential
88. Limited
89. Unsung

Anger:

1. Exploit
2. Money-grubbing
3. Revolting
4. Obnoxious
5. Raise hell
6. Rant
7. Coward

8. Greedy
9. Smug
10. Snotty
11. Snooty
12. Backstabbing
13. Snob
14. Diminish
15. Pound
16. B.S.
17. Pitiful
18. Boil over
19. Arrogant
20. Preposterous
21. Brutal
22. Thug
23. Victim
24. Maul
25. Evil
26. Ruthless
27. Stink
28. Vicious
29. Agitate
30. Sniveling
31. Morally bankrupt
32. Annoy
33. Weak
34. Foul
35. Payback
36. Loser
37. Miff
38. Screw
39. Crooked
40. Bully
41. Violent
42. Hate
43. Worst
44. Provoke

45. Buffoon
46. Know it all
47. Waste
48. Punish
49. No Good
50. Fear
51. Force-fed
52. Corrupt
53. Sneaky
54. Broke
55. Ass kicking
56. Diatribe
57. Bullshit
58. Disgusting
59. Stuck up
60. Loathsome
61. Hostile
62. Lying
63. Lies
64. Beat down
65. Sick and Tired
66. Abuse
67. Underhanded
68. Crush
69. Wounded

Sloth:

1. Mold
2. Gift
3. Painless
4. Simple as ABC
5. Printable
6. No nonsense
7. No sweat
8. Cinch
9. Accessible

10. Uncomplicated
11. Replicate
12. Straightforward
13. Manageable
14. Cheat sheet
15. Light
16. Model
17. List
18. Free
19. Freebie
20. Swipe
21. Economical
22. Efficient
23. Report
24. Comprehensive
25. Mere
26. Snap
27. Basic
28. Instant
29. Guide
30. Factors
31. Smooth
32. Components
33. Steps
34. Steal
35. Downloadable
36. Kickstart
37. How-to
38. Now On demand
39. No problem
40. Ingredients
41. Fail-proof
42. Clear
43. Piece of cake
44. Elements
45. Pattern
46. All-inclusive

47. Index
48. Simple
49. Easy
50. Template
51. Child's play
52. Formula
53. Fill in the blanks
54. Effortless
55. Tools
56. Elementary
57. Picnic
58. Roadmap
59. Building blocks
60. Minutes
61. In record time
62. Quick
63. Ready
64. Copy
65. Complete
66. Plain
67. Smooth sailing
68. Manifest
69. Nothing to it
70. Itemized
71. In less than

Trust:

1. Well respected
2. Don't worry
3. Best
4. Case study
5. Backed
6. Secure
7. According to
8. Lifetime
9. Moneyback

10. No risk
11. Pay zero
12. Guaranteed
13. Scientifically proven
14. Approved
15. Accredited
16. Fully refundable
17. No strings attached
18. Genuine
19. Unconditional
20. Results
21. Try before you buy
22. Best selling
23. Improved
24. Worldwide
25. Authentic
26. No questions asked
27. Studies show
28. Track record
29. Verify
30. Research
31. Safety
32. Recognized
33. Expert
34. Endorsed Ensured
35. Bona fide
36. Ironclad
37. Because
38. No obligation
39. Official
40. Certified
41. Authority
42. Tested

43. Refund
44. Protected
45. Proven
46. Cancel anytime
47. Reliable
48. Professional
49. Anonymous
50. Authoritative
51. Privacy
52. Dependable
53. Recession-proof

Lust:

1. Fascinating
2. Promiscuous
3. Forbidden
4. Sleazy
5. Tantalizing
6. Thrilling
7. Scandalous
8. Riveting
9. Tease
10. Magnetic
11. Lonely
12. Exposed
13. Crave
14. Wanton
15. Tawdry
16. Provocative
17. Sinful
18. Alluring
19. Desire
20. Intriguing
21. Lascivious

22. Engaging
23. Striking
24. Wild
25. Mind-blowing
26. Captivating
27. Steamy
28. Lovely
29. Lust
30. Sleeping
31. Exotic
32. Passionate
33. Pleasurable
34. Lick
35. Mischievous
36. Stimulating
37. Urge
38. Compelling
39. Uncensored
40. Sweaty
41. Dirty
42. Whip
43. Charismatic
44. Obsession
45. Spank
46. Depraved
47. Hypnotic
48. Shameless
49. Naked
50. Flirt
51. Mouthwatering
52. Brazen
53. Enchanting
54. Naughty

Vanity:

1. Gorgeous

2. Mind-blowing
3. Spine
4. Noteworthy
5. Daring
6. Attractive
7. Jubilant
8. Sensational
9. Wealthy
10. Good-looking
11. Moneymaking
12. Bright
13. Valor
14. Turbo charge
15. Notable
16. Conquer
17. Staggering
18. Booming
19. Triumph
20. Dazzling
21. Boost
22. Cheer
23. Victory
24. Wondrous
25. At the top
26. Enchant
27. Guts
28. Brilliant
29. Ahead of the game
30. Fortunate
31. Super-human
32. Strong
33. Effective
34. Elegant
35. Vanquish
36. Defiance
37. Smart
38. Fearless

39. Spectacular
40. Genius
41. Unbeaten
42. Amazing
43. Crowned
44. Successful
45. Foxy
46. Bold
47. Sassy
48. Boss
49. Elite
50. Saucy
51. Prosperous
52. Quick-witted
53. Kick ass
54. Clever
55. Hero
56. Brassy
57. Knockout
58. Beautiful
59. Magic
60. Amplify
61. Bravery
62. Optimal
63. Ultimate
64. Remarkable
65. You
66. Epic
67. Lucky
68. Legendary
69. Awe-inspiring
70. Courage
71. Drop-dead
72. Stunning
73. Jaw-dropping
74. Brazen
75. Wonderful

76. Handsome
77. Undefeated

Made in the USA
Columbia, SC
27 February 2019